BARCELONA Tr... 2023

Vacation to Barcelona made easy with a First-timer Guide, Exploring the hidden gems of Barcelona, tasting the delicious Barcelona's Food.

BY

Michael M. Griffin

All rights reserved. No part of this publication may be reproduced, distributed, or transmitted in any form or by any means, including photocopying, recording, or other electronic or mechanical methods, without the prior written permission of the publisher, except in the case of brief quotations embodied in critical reviews and certain other noncommercial uses permitted by copyright law.

Copyright ©Michael M. Griffin, 2023.

TABLE OF CONTENTS

My trip to Barcelona
Introduction to Barcelona
Brief history of Barcelona
Culture
Religion

Chapter 1: Basic Barcelona Travel Tips

Who should visit Barcelona
Is Barcelona friendly for tourist?
Do I need Visa to enter Barcelona
Barcelona visa requirements
Barcelona Visa fee
When to visit Barcelona
How to get to Barcelona
What to do in Barcelona
What to eat in Barcelona
Barcelona transportation options
where to visit in Barcelona
How long can I stay as a tourist in Barcelona

Chapter 2: what to pack for your vacation
Accessories and Luggages
Medications
Visually Organize confidential information (VPN)
Men outfit wearsWomen outfit wears
Men's foot wear
Women foot wears
Accessorize and toiletries

Chapter 3: Tips for visiting Barcelona at it's best time
Most secured Areas in Barcelona
When is the best time to tour Barcelona cities
Best time to visit Barcelona
The busiest time to visit Barcelona.
Favorite winter location in Barcelona
Barcelona favorite summer location
Proven strategies for locating inexpensive Barcelona flights in Barcelona

The cost of taking the train around Barcelona
The cost of driving or taking a taxi around Barcelona

Chapter 4: What to know before visiting Barcelona as a first timer
Barcelona money
Have some cash at hand
Were to change money in Barcelona
What to know about the Barcelona Sim card suggestion for tourist
Internet and WiFi usage in Barcelona for tourist
Uber and taxi in Barcelona
Dietary restrictions and food
Be cautious in Barcelona
Use of English in Barcelona
Weekend activities in Barcelona
Top 10 money saving tips in Barcelona

Chapter 5: Do's and don't of staying safe in Barcelona
Do not be shy to ask questions
Obey their laws
Careful when crossing the road in Barcelona
Be judicious and watchful
Avoid night movement

Chapter 6: Making friends with Barcelona locals as a tourist
Is Barcelona people friendly and hospitable?
How to mingle with Barcelonians as a tourist
How to approach a Barcelonian

Chapter 7 Best Relaxation and massage center in Barcelona

Chapter 8: Top Barcelona museums

Chapter 9: Top hotels and beaches in Barcelona

Chapter 10: Top Barcelona tourist attraction

My trip to Barcelona

My vacation to Barcelona was a wonderful experience. The dynamic city, situated in the northeastern area of Spain, is famed for its gorgeous architecture, rich cultural history, and wonderful gastronomy.

One of the highlights of my vacation was seeing the famed Sagrada Familia, a cathedral created by the great architect Antoni Gaudi. The rich features and unique style of the cathedral left me in awe.

Another must-visit place in Barcelona is Park Guell, another creation of Gaudi. The park gives panoramic views of the city and is filled with colorful mosaics and sculptures.

Aside from the gorgeous sites, I was also able to immerse myself in the city's rich cultural past by visiting institutions like the Picasso Museum and the Joan Miro Foundation. The museums showcase works by some of Spain's most renowned painters and give an insight into the country's cultural past.

The cuisine in Barcelona was another highlight of my vacation. From the fresh seafood meals to the classic paella, I was able to enjoy a range of exquisite cuisine. The city's markets, such as La Boqueria, are also a must-visit for food enthusiasts, presenting a diversity of local and foreign delights.

my vacation to Barcelona was a magnificent experience that enabled me to enjoy the beauty of the city and its rich cultural legacy. I would highly suggest a visit to anybody seeking to discover a new place.

In addition to the cultural attractions, Barcelona is also recognized for its dynamic atmosphere and buzzing nightlife. During my trip, I got the chance to explore the city's nightlife by visiting some of its famed pubs and clubs. I was delighted by the excitement of the town after dark and was able to dance the night away to the sounds of local DJs.

One of the things I appreciated most about my vacation to Barcelona was its accessibility. The city boasts an extensive public transit infrastructure, making it simple to traverse and explore. I could also wander about the city and uncover hidden beauties along the route. From the street entertainers to the local sellers, I was able to absorb the colorful vibe of the city.

Another feature of Barcelona that I admired was its rich history. The city is deep in history, from its Roman beginnings to its medieval history, and I was able to learn so much about the city's past by visiting its numerous historical sites and museums.

In conclusion, my vacation to Barcelona was a fantastic experience. The city's beauty, cultural depth, and energetic atmosphere made it an ideal location for my trips. I would strongly suggest a visit to anybody eager to experience a new place full of history, art, and vivacious energy.

Additionally, I was able to explore the local culture in Barcelona by engaging with the kind inhabitants. They were always happy to assist and offer their expertise about the city. I was also able to enjoy classic Spanish cuisine, such as tapas and sangria, which contributed to my whole experience.

Another great experience was visiting the Gothic Quarter, where I was able to meander around the tiny alleyways surrounded by old buildings and beautiful cafés. The Gothic Quarter is a must-visit for anybody interested in the city's medieval heritage.

Barcelona is also a shopper's paradise, providing a wide variety of shopping possibilities, from high-end shops to local markets. I was able to bring back unique mementos, such as handmade pottery and jewelry, as a memory of my vacation.

In conclusion, my vacation to Barcelona was a wonderful experience that I will enjoy for a lifetime. The city has plenty to offer everyone, from its rich cultural past to its energetic environment, making it a must-visit location. I can't wait to plan my next vacation to this great city

Brief history of Barcelona

Barcelona is the capital of Catalonia in Spain and has a rich history stretching back to the Roman era. During the Middle Ages, it was an important economic town and played a major role in the Gothic architecture movement. During the 19th and 20th centuries, Barcelona underwent considerable development and renovation, which culminated in its hosting of the 1992 Summer Olympics. Throughout its history, Barcelona has been a centre for art, culture, and politics, making it one of the most known cities in Spain and a popular tourist destination.

Culture

Barcelona, the capital of Catalonia, is famous for its rich cultural past. Some of the cultural highlights of the city include:

Architecture: Barcelona is known for its modernist architecture, notably the works of Antoni Gaudí such as Park Güell, CASA Batlló and La Sagrada Familia.

Art: The city is home to many art museums, including the Joan Miro Foundation, the Picasso Museum and the National Art Museum of Catalonia.

Food: Barcelona boasts a rich and diverse culinary scene, with traditional Catalan food and a range of international choices.

Festivals and events: Barcelona conducts various cultural events throughout the year, such as La Mercè (the city's main festival), the Barcelona Beach Festival, and the Barcelona International Jazz Festival.

Sports: Barcelona is also famous for its excitement for sports, mainly soccer, with FC Barcelona being one of the most successful and popular football teams in the world.

Religion

Spain is a culturally varied city with a long past, and its religious makeup reflects that variety. The predominant religion in Barcelona is Roman Catholicism, followed by a substantial number of persons who identify as irreligious or atheist. Other religions represented in the city include Protestantism, Orthodox Christianity, Judaism, and Islam.

Chapter 1: Basic Barcelona Travel Tip

Who should visit Barcelona

Anyone who is interested in history, art, architecture, gastronomy, and culture should consider visiting Barcelona. It is a city with a rich history, magnificent architecture, wonderful food, and dynamic cultural scene. It provides a unique combination of ancient sites, like as the Sagrada Familia, Park Guell, and Gothic Quarter, as well as contemporary attractions like the beach, nightlife, and shopping. Whether you are traveling single, with family, or companions, Barcelona provides something for everyone.

Barcelona is a popular destination for sports enthusiasts, since it is home to one of the world's most recognized football teams, FC Barcelona. The city also boasts a booming nighttime culture with lots of pubs, clubs, and restaurants to pick from.

Barcelona is a hotspot for art and design, with iconic works by Antoni Gaudi, Joan Miro, and Pablo Picasso on show in local museums. Finally, the city is surrounded by natural beauty, with the Costa Brava and Pyrenees Mountains both within driving distance, making it a perfect location for outdoor lovers. Overall, Barcelona provides something for everyone, making it a must-visit location.

Is Barcelona friendly for tourist?

Barcelona is a pleasant city for travelers. The city is widely recognized for its warm attitude and rich cultural legacy, drawing millions of tourists every year. There are numerous tourist-friendly services, including a well-developed public transit system, a vast choice of food options, and many tourist sites and places to explore.

The residents of Barcelona are typically cordial and courteous towards visitors. They are proud of their city and its rich history, and are delighted to share it with guests. The city also offers a busy nightlife, with lots of pubs, clubs, and other entertainment alternatives to suit diverse interests and budgets. Overall, Barcelona is a terrific location for travelers who are searching for a blend of culture, history, and pleasure.

However, it is always crucial for travelers to be aware of their surroundings and to take the required safety measures, particularly while visiting unknown regions. This is true for every large city, and Barcelona is no exception. It is also crucial to respect the local norms and culture, and to be cautious of your actions in public settings.

Barcelona is a pleasant and inviting city for travelers, giving a multitude of opportunity to explore its rich cultural history, enjoy its numerous attractions and sites, and take part in its dynamic nightlife. With a little amount of common sense and prudence, tourists to Barcelona may have a safe and pleasurable experience.

Do I need Visa to enter Barcelona?

It depends on your place of origin and the length of your stay. If you are a citizen of the European Union (EU), European Economic Area (EEA) or Switzerland, you may visit Barcelona without a visa and remain for up to 90 days without having to apply for any extra permissions. However, if you are a citizen of a nation outside of the EU, you may need a visa, depending on the duration and purpose of your trip. It is important to verify the precise visa requirements for your country with the Spanish embassy or consulate.

It is also crucial to remember that owing to the COVID-19 epidemic, there may be extra entrance restrictions or procedures in place for both EU and non-EU persons. For example, you may need to show a negative COVID-19 test result or quarantine upon arrival. It is essential to verify the latest information on entrance requirements before coming to Barcelona, since these laws might change often.

A visa for Spain is a document that permits you to enter and remain in the country for a set amount of time and for a particular reason, such as tourism, study, job, or family reunion. The kind of visa you require and the application procedure will vary based on the duration of your stay and the purpose for your visit.
whether or not you need a visa to visit Barcelona depends on your place of origin and the purpose of your travel. It is important to verify the current visa requirements with the Spanish embassy or consulate before visiting.

It is also crucial to have all the appropriate documentation in order, such as a valid passport or national ID card, travel insurance, and evidence of financial resources to support your stay in Spain. It is essential to have all the relevant papers ready and arranged before submitting your visa application to prevent any delays or issues throughout the procedure.

Once you arrive in Barcelona, it is important to educate yourself about local traditions and regulations and to comply with all Spanish laws. This will ensure that your stay in Barcelona is safe, enjoyable, and memorable.

If you are expecting to remain in Spain for a lengthy amount of time, it is vital to consider registering with the local authorities and acquiring a Spanish ID card or residence permit. This will enable you to access local services and benefits and will ease many elements of everyday living in Spain.

In conclusion, obtaining the relevant visa and essential papers is a vital step in planning for a successful trip to Barcelona. By taking the time to study and comply with all requirements, you can guarantee that your stay in Spain is seamless and stress-free

Barcelona visa requirements

travelers visiting Barcelona, Spain from most countries including the US, Canada, Australia, and many European nations are needed to have a valid passport but do not need a visa for stays up to 90 days for tourism or business reasons.
However, it's always advisable to check with the Spanish embassy in your country or the immigration authorities in Spain for the most up-to-date information, since visa requirements sometimes vary.

Additionally, if you want to remain in Spain for longer than 90 days or plan to work or study in the country, you may need to apply for a longer-term visa. The kind of visa needed will depend on the exact conditions of your travel, such as your purpose of visit, duration of stay, and job or study intentions. It's essential to remember that visitors from certain countries may still need a visa regardless of the duration of stay, so it's always wise to verify the precise rules for your place of origin.

To apply for a visa, you may need to supply paperwork such as a passport, proof of financial support, health insurance, and evidence of your purpose of travel. Acquiring a visa might take many weeks or months, so it's crucial to prepare early if you're planning a trip to Spain.

Barcelona Visa fee

The visa fee for Barcelona, Spain varies depending on the type of visa you are applying for and your country of origin. As of my knowledge cut-off lately, here are the approximate visa fees for some common types of visas:

Schengen Tourist Visa: 60 EUR
National Long-Stay Visa: 300 EUR
Student Visa: 60 EUR

It's important to note that these fees are subject to change and may vary based on your specific circumstances. You can check the most up-to-date information by contacting the Spanish embassy or consulate in your country or the immigration authorities in Spain. Additionally, some applicants may be required to pay additional fees for processing or administrative costs.

It's also important to keep in mind that visa fees are non-refundable, even if your visa application is denied. This means that it's crucial to make sure you have all the required documentation and meet the eligibility criteria before submitting your application.

If you're planning a trip to Barcelona, it's always best to check the most up-to-date information on visa requirements and fees well in advance of your trip. This will give you enough time to gather the necessary documentation and ensure that you have everything in order before you travel.

It's worth noting that some countries offer visa-free travel for short-term stays for citizens of certain countries, so you may be able to travel to Barcelona without a visa, depending on your country of origin. Be sure to check the specific requirements for your country of origin before making travel plans.

When to visit Barcelona

As a first-timer, the ideal time to visit Barcelona is from March to May or from September to November. During these months, the weather is temperate and pleasant, and the crowds are significantly lower compared to the peak tourist season (July-August) (July-August). Additionally, you'll get the option to witness local celebrations such as La Mercè, a traditional festival celebrated in September.

However, if you like warm weather and are fine with heavier people, then the months of July and August are also perfect to come. During these months, the city comes alive with street entertainment, beach activities, and open-air concerts.

Regardless matter when you arrive, Barcelona has lots to offer. You may tour the famed masterpieces of Antoni Gaudí, including the Sagrada Familia and Park Güell, visit the Gothic Quarter for an insight into the city's past, or enjoy the local cuisine. And if you're a lover of art, don't miss out on the Picasso Museum or Joan Miro Foundation.

The ideal time to visit Barcelona varies on your interests, although the city is a beautiful vacation year-round.

Regardless of the season, it's always a good idea to plan your vacation and make reservations for famous sights, particularly during peak tourist season. This will guarantee that you have a hassle-free and pleasurable experience.

Another piece of advice for visiting Barcelona is to take use of the public transit system, which includes buses, trains, and the metro. It's an easy and economical method to go about the city and explore its numerous sights and attractions.

Don't forget to immerse yourself in the local culture by sampling the typical Catalan food, visiting a local market, or participating in a Flamenco performance. These encounters will give you a greater respect for the city and its lively culture.

Barcelona is a lively and dynamic city with a rich history, culture, and gastronomy. Whether you come in the spring, summer, autumn, or winter, you're guaranteed to have an outstanding time.

How to get to Barcelona
Barcelona

There are various methods to reach Barcelona:

1.By Plane: Barcelona's principal airport is El Prat International Airport, which provides flights from many important cities worldwide.

2.By Railway: Barcelona has multiple train stations, notably Estació de França and Estació Sants, with regular trains linking the city to other regions of Spain and Europe.

3.By Bus: Barcelona is serviced by various long-distance bus companies, giving links to other cities in Spain and Europe.

4.By Automobile: Barcelona may be accessed by car through many routes, notably the AP-7, which runs along the Mediterranean coast.

5.By Cruise: Barcelona is a popular port of call for Mediterranean cruise ships.

Once you have arrived in Barcelona, there are various alternatives for traveling about the city, including:

1.Public Transportation: The city boasts a large network of buses, trams, and metro lines, making it simple to move about without a vehicle.

2.Taxis: Taxis are frequently accessible and may be hailed on the street or at taxi stands.

3.Bicycles: Barcelona has a bike-sharing scheme called Bicing, which lets residents and tourists ride bikes for short excursions throughout the city.

4.Walking: Many of Barcelona's tourist sites are situated inside the city center, making it convenient to explore on foot.

5.Cars: If you prefer to drive, you may hire a vehicle from one of the numerous rental firms situated in the city. However, be warned that traffic in Barcelona may be heavy and parking might be challenging to locate.

Regardless matter how you choose to travel, Barcelona is a dynamic city with a rich history, gorgeous architecture, and a busy cultural scene, making it a must-visit destination for tourists from across the globe.

What to do in Barcelona:

Barcelona is a dynamic city with many things to see and do. Here are some prominent tourist sites and activities:
1. Visit the Sagrada Familia - the renowned church created by Antoni Gaudi.
2. Walk down Las Ramblas – a busy boulevard packed with street performers, shops, and cafés.
3. Explore Park Güell - another masterpiece of Gaudi, including mosaic-covered buildings and stunning vistas of the city.
4. Visit the Gothic Quarter - the medieval quarter of Barcelona with small alleys, squares, and ancient structures.
5. See the Picasso Museum - devoted to the works of the great Spanish artist, Pablo Picasso.

6. Enjoy the beach - Barcelona is famed for its beaches, such as Barceloneta and Nova Icaria.

7. Try local food - taste classic meals like paella and tapas at one of the numerous restaurants in the city.

8. Visit the Palau de la Música Catalana – a beautiful modernist music venue.

9. Shop at the La Boqueria Market – a lively market offering food, flowers, and gifts.

10. Take a day trip to Montserrat - a picturesque mountain range and a popular site for trekking and sightseeing.

11. Visit Casa Batlló and Casa Milà - two of Antoni Gaudi's iconic architectural creations, notable for their distinctive design and ornamentation.

12. Stroll through Ciutadella Park - a big park with a lake, a zoo, and various museums and galleries.

13. Explore the Gothic Cathedral - the Cathedral of the Holy Cross and Saint Eulalia, a majestic gothic cathedral in the center of the city.

14.Take a Flamenco performance - witness the passion and fire of Flamenco, a historic Spanish dance genre.

15.Visit the Joan Miro Foundation - a museum devoted to the works of the great Spanish artist Joan Miro.

16.Take a culinary tour - experience the local cuisine and learn about the history and culture of Barcelona via its food.

17.Visit the Magic Fountain of Montjuic - a stunning water and light performance set against the background

What to eat in Barcelona:

Barcelona is recognized for its rich culinary history and provides a broad choice of foods and cuisine types to experience. Some must-try foods in Barcelona include:

Paella: a typical Valencian rice meal that comes in numerous forms including seafood, mixed and vegetarian.

Gazpacho: a cold soup comprised of tomato, cucumber, peppers, and bread that is popular in the summer.

Tapas: tiny plates of food that are generally paired with beverages and are a terrific way to experience a range of Spanish cuisines.

Calçots: a sort of green onion that is grilled and served with a spicy tomato sauce.

Churros with chocolate: a traditional Spanish morning food, fried dough pastry served with a warm cup of rich chocolate for dipping.

Patatas bravas: fried potatoes paired with a spicy tomato sauce.

Bocadillo de calamares: a typical sandwich prepared with fried squid and served on a baguette.

Where to consume these delicacies is subject to personal taste, however, there are numerous historic restaurants in the city that provide true Catalan cuisine.

Barcelona is also a city that welcomes new food, so many contemporary restaurants give a fresh perspective on classic meals. For example, you may discover fusion tapas bars that blend Spanish ingredients with tastes from various cuisines, such as Asian or Mediterranean.

In addition to sit-down restaurants, there are several food markets in Barcelona where you can enjoy fresh local products and experience street cuisine. La Boqueria, situated near La Rambla, is one of the most renowned markets in the city and is an excellent spot to experience local delicacies.

Regarding beverages, Barcelona is famed for its sangria, a fruity wine-based cocktail that is a mainstay of Spanish cuisine. Cava, a sparkling wine manufactured in Catalonia, is also a popular drink to sample while in Barcelona.

Overall, there is no lack of wonderful food and drink to enjoy in Barcelona, so don't be afraid to be brave and try new things!

Barcelona transportation options

There are various transit choices in Barcelona:

Metro: The metro system is the most convenient method to commute inside the city. It has 11 lines and covers most regions of the city.
2.Bus: The bus network is broad and reaches places not covered by the metro.

3.Tram: Trams run in various sections of the city and are a nice alternative for going along the beach.

4.Taxis: Taxis are frequently accessible and may be hailed on the street or ordered in advance.

5.Bicing: This is Barcelona's public bike-sharing system, which enables you to borrow a bike for short rides.

6.Walking: Barcelona is a walkable city and many tourist sites are within walking distance of each other.

7.Rental Vehicle: Renting a car is an option, however, traffic and parking may be an issue in the city center.

8. Aerobus: This is a shuttle bus service that links Barcelona El Prat Airport with the city center.It operates every 5-10 minutes and is a quick and easy method to commute to and from the airport.

8.Railway : Various train stations in Barcelona link the city to other regions of Catalonia and Spain.

9.Cable Car: The Cable Car (Telefèric de Montjuïc) gives panoramic views of the city and provides a direct link between the Montjuïc castle and the port.

All of these transit methods are reasonable, except taxis, and may be readily accessible with a multi-day travel pass or single-use ticket. Barcelona's public transit system is well-organized and dependable, making it simple to navigate throughout the city and reach your chosen locations

where to visit Barcelona

Here are some notable tourist sites in Barcelona that you may visit:

Sagrada Familia - the landmark cathedral created by Antoni Gaudis Park Guell - a park with vivid mosaics and sculptures by Antoni Gaudi
Casa Batllo – a modernist structure created by Antoni Gaudi
La Rambla - a thoroughfare famed for shopping, restaurants, and street performers

Gothic Quarter– a historic district with small lanes and structures from medieval times

Picasso Museum - devoted to the works of Pablo Picasso

Palau de la Musica Catalana - a performance venue notable for its unusual modernist architecture.

Camp Nou – the stadium of the famed Barcelona Football Club

La Boqueria - one of the greatest food marketplaces in Europe

Barcelona Cathedral – a Gothic cathedral in the Gothic Quarter

These are only some of the numerous things to visit in the city, and there is much more to explore.

Additionally, if you're interested in art and architecture, there are numerous additional structures in the city constructed by Antoni Gaudi that are worth seeing, such as the **Casa Mila and the Palau Guell.**

For those interested in history, **the History Museum of Catalonia** is an excellent site to learn about the history of the area. The museum is set in the old Royal Palace of Catalonia and has exhibits on the medieval and contemporary eras of Catalan history.

For nature enthusiasts, **Ciutadella Park** is a lovely park in the middle of the city with a huge lake, fountains, and various statues. The park also features a small zoo and a boating lake where you may hire a boat and go for a row.

Lastly, for a sense of the local culture, a visit to the **El Born area** is a must. This attractive district is dotted with tiny stores, cafés, and restaurants, and is noted for its vibrant atmosphere and cultural history.

Barcelona is a city with lots to offer and these are just a handful of the many things you may see and do while you're here.

How long can I stay as a tourist in Barcelona

As a tourist, the length of time you can stay in Barcelona depends on your nationality and the country that issued your passport. If you are a citizen of a country within the European Union (EU), you can stay in Spain, including Barcelona, for an unlimited period of time. If you are a citizen of a country outside the EU, the maximum length of time you can stay as a tourist is 90 days within a 180-day period. This means that you can spend a maximum of 90 days in Spain within a 6-month period, and then you must leave the country for at least 90 days before coming back as a tourist again. Please note that these are general guidelines, and immigration authorities have the final say on the length of time you can stay in Spain.

It's important to keep in mind that the length of time you are allowed to stay as a tourist in Barcelona is not the same as the length of time you can legally work or study there. If you plan to stay in Barcelona for a longer period of time, you may need to obtain a work or study visa before you arrive. Additionally, if you plan to stay for an extended period of time, you may also need to meet other requirements, such as obtaining health insurance or registering with local authorities.

It's always a good idea to check the latest travel advice from your country's government and the Spanish government before traveling to Barcelona. This information can help you ensure that you have all the necessary documents and information to stay in the country legally and safely.

The length of time you can stay in Barcelona as a tourist depends on your nationality and the country that issued your passport. As a general rule, citizens of the EU can stay in Spain for an unlimited period of time, while citizens of non-EU countries can stay for a maximum of 90 days within a 180-day period. Before traveling to Barcelona, it's important to check the latest travel advice and requirements to ensure that you have a safe and enjoyable trip.

It's also worth mentioning that while in Barcelona, you should abide by the laws and regulations of Spain. This includes respecting local customs and traditions, as well as following rules related to things like traffic and public behavior. Being familiar with local laws and regulations can help ensure that you have a positive experience while visiting Barcelona.

It's crucial to be prepared for your vacation. This includes possessing a valid passport or other travel documentation, as well as having enough money to pay your expenditures while you are in the nation. You should also educate yourself with the local language, currency, and other crucial facts about Barcelona before you come, so that you are well-prepared for your vacation. In summary, there are numerous variables to consider while arranging a trip to Barcelona as a tourist. From knowing the amount of time you may remain in the nation, to being aware of local laws and traditions, to being prepared for your trip, there are many things to keep in mind to ensure that you have a safe and happy visit. With the correct preparation and attention to detail, you can make the most of your time in Barcelona.

Chapter 2: Travel Preparation

what to bring with you as a tourist.

When preparing for a vacation, there are a few different factors.

Place: What you should bring will depend on the sort of destination you are visiting. For instance, you'll need sandals, sunscreen, and swimwear if you're going to a beach.

You will need warm gear, such as a coat, gloves, and a hat if you are traveling in a cooler area.

Thinking about your intended itinerary activities can help you pack wisely.

You will need the correct gear and equipment whether you wish to go trekking or spend time at the beach.

Length of stay: Take into consideration how long your journey will be and pack appropriately. You'll need to pack more clothes and toiletries if you'll be gone for a long period.

Bring any personal goods you may need, such as prescription prescriptions, eyeglasses or contact lenses, and devices like phone and laptops.

Making a list of the goods you need to pack before you start packing is typically a good idea. This will make it easy for you to remember everything you need and guarantee that you don't neglect anything crucial.

Accessories and Luggages to consider bringing.

When going to Barcelona, it is vital to pack carefully and carry needed items and baggage to make your vacation more comfortable and pleasurable. Some suggested things to carry include:

A decent-quality backpack or shoulder bag to carry your necessities throughout the day.

Comfortable shoes for strolling and visiting the city.

A waterproof jacket or umbrella, since the weather in Barcelona, may be unpredictable. Portable charger or power bank keeps your phone or other gadgets charged.

A water bottle to remain hydrated while visiting the city.
Travel adapter to charge your electronics at a different electrical outlet.
A camera to record your moments in Barcelona.
A daypack or a tote bag for any purchases or extra goods throughout the day.
A baggage lock to safeguard your stuff at your hotel or hostel.
A travel cushion for long flights or train excursions.

Overall, it's ideal to travel light and pick adaptable products that may be worn or utilized in various ways to conserve room and make your vacation more pleasant

In terms of baggage, it is necessary to evaluate the sort of trip you will be conducting and the duration of your stay. For shorter travels, a carry-on size suitcase or duffel bag should be adequate. For longer trips or if you intend on doing a lot of shopping, bigger checked luggage may be essential. When purchasing a suitcase, seek for one with durable wheels, a comfortable handle, and a solid build to safeguard your possessions throughout travel. A suitcase with several compartments may also help you keep your belongings organized and readily accessible.

It is also a good idea to pack a lightweight and collapsible tote or shopping bag to serve as an extra piece of baggage or to carry products during your travels. This might come in helpful if you need to transport goods that do not fit in your main baggage, such as souvenirs or shopping purchases.

Overall, the key to packing for a vacation to Barcelona is to include goods that will make your trip comfortable and pleasurable but also being cautious of the weight and size of your baggage. By picking the correct accessories and baggage, you can guarantee that your vacation to Barcelona is a success.

Medications idea for Barcelona vacation

If you are heading to Barcelona and have any special medical issues, it is always important to contact your healthcare professional before visiting. They may suggest suitable drugs and treatments that you may require throughout your vacation.

However, here are a few broad tips for typical travel-related health concerns:

Motion sickness: Over-the-counter drugs such as Dramamine or ginger may assist with motion nausea.

Jet lag: Melatonin, a natural hormone, may be used to assist adjust sleep patterns while flying between time zones.

Allergies: Over-the-counter antihistamines such as Benadryl may be used to reduce allergy symptoms.

Pain treatment: Over-the-counter pain relief drugs such as Tylenol or Advil may be used to reduce headaches, muscular pains, and other forms of pain.

Diarrhea: Over-the-counter drugs such as Imodium may be used to aid with symptoms of traveler's diarrhea.

It is also necessary to have a first-aid kit containing basic materials such as band-aids, gauze, antiseptic wipes, and any prescription prescriptions you may require.

Here are some important considerations for your vacation to Barcelona:

Sun protection: Make sure to pack a high-SPF sunscreen and protective gear to prevent the sun's damaging rays, particularly during the summer months.
Hydration: Stay hydrated by drinking lots of water and avoiding alcohol and caffeine, which may dehydrate the body.
Mosquito protection: If you are going to places where mosquito-borne illnesses are a concern, pack insect repellent and consider wearing long sleeves and slacks to reduce skin exposure.
Vaccines: Check with your healthcare physician or a travel medicine clinic to learn whether any vaccinations are recommended for your trip to Barcelona. Some typical travel immunizations are Hepatitis A, Typhoid, and Rabies.

Remember, these are just broad tips and it is crucial to speak with a healthcare expert for individualized advice and treatment recommendations based on your unique health requirements and travel plans. Safe travels!

Visually Organize confidential information (VPN) for a trip to Barcelona

Here's one method you may visually arrange your personal information for a trip to Barcelona:

Create a folder titled "Barcelona Trip" on your computer or in the cloud.

Within the folder, create a document named "VPN Information."

In the VPN Information document, list the following information:

VPN service provider name

Login credentials (username and password) (username and password)
Server location(s) to be utilized in Barcelona
Save the document and password-protect it for further protection.

If you prefer a physical copy, print the VPN Information sheet and put it in a secure location, such as a locked file cabinet or a hotel safe.
Consider utilizing a password manager to securely store your VPN credentials and other sensitive information.

By graphically arranging your secret information, you may immediately retrieve it when required and avoid the danger of losing or disclosing important information when traveling.
In addition to the VPN Information document, you may create a document titled "Important Contact Information." This might include:

Emergency contact information (such as the phone number of your embassy in Barcelona) (such as the phone number of your embassy in Barcelona)

Phone numbers and email addresses of relatives or friends you will be traveling with

Phone numbers and email addresses of any hotels or restaurants you have booked

You may also create a document titled "Trip Itinerary" that summarizes your travel arrangements, including:

Flight information (flight numbers, departure and arrival times, carriers) (flight numbers, departure and arrival times, airlines)

Hotel reservations

Any scheduled activities or vacations

Store all of these papers under the "Barcelona Trip" folder for quick access.

Make sure to routinely back up your "Barcelona Trip" folder to an external hard drive or cloud storage provider to guarantee that your information is protected even if your device is lost or stolen.

By following these procedures, you may successfully arrange and safeguard your personal information when going to Barcelona.

Barcelona Outfit Suggestions for a trip to Barcelona

guys might consider wearing comfortable and attractive apparel such as:

Lightweight linen or cotton pants
Short-sleeve or long-sleeve button-up shirts in breathable fabrics
Comfortable sneakers or loafers
A light jacket or sweater for chilly nights
A hat to shield against the sun
Sunglasses
It's also vital to consider the season and weather conditions while packing.

In terms of style, Barcelona is noted for its fashion-forward, laid-back atmosphere. So, you may select a casual, but refined design that still provides comfort throughout your trips. You may match your shirt with tailored shorts or chinos for a more dressed-up appearance, or keep it casual with a t-shirt and jeans.

When it comes to footwear, comfy shoes or loafers are perfect for visiting the city, since you'll likely be doing a lot of walking. If you intend on doing any sightseeing, be sure you choose shoes that give appropriate support and cushioning.

Additionally, because Barcelona is situated near the shore, it's a good idea to carry a light jacket or sweater for chilly nights, particularly if you're going in the spring or autumn. A hat and sunglasses are also vital to protect oneself from the sun, particularly during the hot

Barcelona Outfit Suggestions for Ladies

For a vacation to Barcelona, ladies may bring a choice of costumes that are both beautiful and comfortable. Here are some suggestions:

Light summer clothing - for sunny days and visiting tourist sites

Denim shorts and a breezy shirt - informal and comfy for touring the city

Linen trousers with a tank top - for a more put-together appearance

A skirt and blouse - for a more sophisticated appearance in the evenings

Comfortable walking shoes - for touring the city on foot

It's usually a good idea to check the weather prediction before packing and to bring clothes for cold nights.

Men's footwear choices for a vacation to Barcelona

When going to Barcelona, it is advisable to carry comfortable and adaptable shoes for walking and touring. A pair of sneakers or casual loafers might be fine, particularly if you intend on doing a lot of walking. If you're traveling during the summer, sandals or espadrilles might also be a wonderful alternative. Avoid wearing heavy hiking boots or shoes that are tough to walk in, since you will be doing a lot of walking and touring in this city.

Additionally, if you intend on visiting any of the city's famed architectural monuments, such as Gaudi's Park Guell or La Sagrada Familia, it's crucial to wear shoes that give sufficient support, since you'll be climbing stairs and walking on uneven terrain. Additionally, if you intend on eating at upmarket restaurants or visiting any high-end shopping districts, it's a good idea to pack a pair of dressier shoes, such as oxfords or loafers, to blend in with the local fashion sense.

Remember to carefully consider the weather while packing your shoes. If you're traveling during the warmer months, be sure to pack breathable shoes to keep your feet cool, while in the colder months, you may want to bring shoes with additional insulation and protection from the elements.

In conclusion, while coming to Barcelona, it's ideal for carrying comfortable and adaptable shoes that can take a lot of walking and touring, as well as a pair of dressier shoes for more upmarket situations. Make sure to evaluate the weather and the activities you intend on performing and bring shoes that are suited for those scenarios.

Women's Vacation Footwear ideas for a trip to Barcelona

When going to Barcelona, ladies might consider wearing comfortable and attractive shoes for the numerous activities they intend on undertaking. Good alternatives include sneakers for a casual style while wandering about the city, sandals for a sunny day at the beach, and loafers or flats for a more elegant look for visiting museums or historic buildings. It's crucial to take in mind the terrain and the weather since certain streets might be uneven and rainy days are prevalent in the city.

It's also a good idea to take a pair of waterproof shoes or boots in case of unexpected weather. Additionally, Barcelona is renowned for its nightlife and eating scene, so ladies may want to bring a pair of dressier shoes for a night out. Whether you're touring the Gothic Quarter, visiting Park Güell, or shopping on Passeig Gracia, having the correct footwear can assist guarantee a pleasant and pleasurable vacation to Barcelona. Don't forget to also take socks and foot inserts if you have any foot sensitivity. Overall, it's advisable to bring a selection of shoes to fit your schedule and be prepared for any circumstance.

When picking footwear for a vacation to Barcelona, it's also vital to consider the cultural norms and dress regulations of the city. Barcelona is recognized for being a fashion-forward city, and many inhabitants dress elegantly even while merely doing errands or going for a stroll. Wearing shoes that are both comfortable and trendy will not only make your vacation more fun, but will also help you fit in with the locals and feel confident while visiting the city.

Finally, it's crucial to remember that Barcelona is a city with a lot of walking, so it's necessary to put comfort above style. Make careful to break in any new shoes before your vacation and pack band-aids and blister pads in case you need them. A successful vacation to Barcelona involves not just the appropriate footwear, but also a little bit of planning and foresight.

Barcelona Trip Accessories Toiletries

For a vacation to Barcelona, consider carrying the following goods for accessories and toiletries:
Sunglasses, Sunscreen, Hat, Scarf, wrap,
Comfortable walking shoes
Camera
Portable charger
Toiletries: toothbrush, toothpaste, shampoo, conditioner, moisturizer, lip balm, and any personal prescriptions.
Note: It's always a good idea to check the weather forecast and prepare appropriately.

Additionally, Barcelona is recognized for its beautiful weather and cultural attractions, so consider bringing:
Light, airy apparel for hot weather
Comfortable attire for touring the city
Swimwear for the beach or pool
Reusable water bottle
Light jacket or sweater for chilly nights
Cash and/or travel credit card
Travel adaptor for charging electronics

Portable umbrella in case of rain.

Chapter 3: Tips for visiting Barcelona at it's best time

Most secured Areas in Barcelona for tourist

Barcelona is a safe city for tourists, but as with any large city, it's always wise to take precautions to protect yourself and your belongings. Here are some of the most secure areas in Barcelona for tourists:

El Raval: This neighborhood is located near the Gothic Quarter and is considered to be one of the safest areas in Barcelona. It is well-policed and has a low crime rate.

Gothic Quarter: The Gothic Quarter is a historic neighborhood that is popular with tourists. It is well-lit, has plenty of pedestrian traffic, and is patrolled by police.

Eixample: This neighborhood is known for its wide, tree-lined boulevards and is considered to be one of the safest areas in Barcelona.

Gracia: Gracia is a bohemian neighborhood that is popular with tourists. It has a low crime rate and is well-policed.

Barceloneta: This neighborhood is located near the beach and is a popular destination for tourists. It is well-lit and has a low crime rate.

Remember to always keep an eye on your belongings, be aware of your surroundings, and use common sense when exploring the city.

Additionally, here are some general safety tips for tourists in Barcelona:

Avoid walking alone in dark and deserted areas, especially at night.

Keep precious valuables, such as passports and money, in a hotel safe or a money belt worn under clothes.

Be cautious of pickpocketing, especially in tourist areas, crowded markets, and on public transportation.

Avoid displaying expensive jewelry or electronic devices, as these can attract the attention of pickpockets and thieves.

Stay in well-lit and busy areas, especially when returning to your hotel or accommodation late at night.

Always be aware of your surroundings and avoid wearing headphones or glancing at your phone in public, since this might make you more susceptible to theft.

If you need assistance, seek help from a police officer or a hotel staff member.

Barcelona is a wonderful city that attracts millions of tourists every year, and with a little caution and common sense, you can ensure a safe and enjoyable trip.

When is the best time to tour Barcelona cities

Tourist season. However, it ultimately depends on personal choice and what you would want to experience during your stay since Barcelona boasts events and celebrations year-round.

Barcelona is a city with a rich cultural legacy and is noted for its gorgeous architecture, museums, and beaches. Summer is the busiest time of year for travelers, with temperatures averaging in the mid-70s to 80s Fahrenheit. Despite the throngs, the city comes alive throughout the summer months with street festivals, open-air music, and beach parties. Winter is the quietest season in Barcelona, with warm temperatures and fewer people, however, certain sites may have shortened hours or be closed entirely. Regardless of when you visit, Barcelona is a city that provides something for everyone, and the ideal time to explore will depend on your unique interests and travel objectives.

Best time to visit Barcelona

The ideal season to visit Barcelona is from late spring to early fall, from May to September, when the weather is mild and pleasant with average temperatures ranging from 20°C to 30°C. During this month, various outdoor events and activities take place, making it the peak tourist season. However, if you want to avoid crowds and have more monetary flexibility, going during the winter months might also be a fantastic alternative, with moderate weather and fewer people.

However, if you want to travel during the busy season, it's best to book lodgings and activities well in advance since costs tend to be higher and availability may be restricted.

Aside from the weather, Barcelona also provides various cultural and historical sites, such as the Sagrada Familia, Park Güell, and the Gothic Quarter. The city also features dynamic nightlife and a famous culinary scene, with numerous pubs, restaurants, and markets to visit.

No matter what time of year you come, Barcelona has something to offer everyone. Whether you're wanting to soak up the sun on the beach, discover the city's rich history and culture, or just taste the local food, you're sure to have an entertaining and unforgettable vacation.

The busiest time to visit Barcelona.

The busiest time to visit Barcelona is during the summer months (July and August) as well as during holiday times such as Christmas and Easter. Additionally, events like the La Mercè festival and the Barcelona

Beach festival also tend to draw enormous audiences.

During these peak seasons, tourist sites and popular neighborhoods including La Rambla, Park Guell, and the Gothic Quarter may get packed, resulting in lengthier wait times and a less pleasurable experience. If you're seeking to escape the crowds, it may be better to schedule your vacation to Barcelona during the spring or autumn months when fewer visitors are visiting the city. However, bear in mind that these seasons might sometimes bring colder weather, so be careful to prepare appropriately. Regardless matter when you come, be prepared to enjoy the rich culture, history, and gastronomy that make Barcelona a renowned tourist destination.

Favorite winter location in Barcelona

There is no single winter spot that is widely regarded as the favorite in Barcelona since it relies on personal tastes and interests. However, some popular winter spots in Barcelona include:

Park Güell - A public park built by Antoni Gaudi, affording panoramic views of the city and a quirky combination of architecture and nature.

Casa Batlló - A modernist architecture constructed by Antoni Gaudi, famed for its magnificent exterior and unusual architectural characteristics.

La Rambla - A lively boulevard and renowned tourist attraction, dotted with street entertainers, stores, and cafés.

La Boqueria Market - One of the biggest food markets in Europe, providing a varied choice of fresh fruit, meats, and local delicacies.

Basilica de la Sagrada Familia - An remarkable temple constructed by Antoni Gaudi, noted for its distinctive architecture and beautiful sculptures.

favorite summertime destination for First-Timers

Barcelona is a well-liked travel destination renowned for its magnificent architecture, extensive cultural heritage, and energetic environment. Tourists may enjoy a variety of stunning locales throughout the summer. Barcelona's most well-liked summertime vacation spots include:

The most well-known beach in the city is Barceloneta Beach, which is a must-see location in the summer. It's a wonderful location for enjoying the sun, the sea, and some delectable seafood.

The famed architect Antoni Gaud created the quirky Park Güell, which is a wonderful spot to unwind and take in the cityscape. Additionally, picnics and picture ops are common there.

La Rambla: This renowned avenue, one of the most well-known in the city, is dotted with cafés, stores, and street performers. It's a terrific location for people-watching and taking in the city's bustle.

The Mountaintop fortification known as Montjuc Castle is a wonderful spot to escape the heat and take in the city's breathtaking vistas. It's a well-liked location for watching the sun set.

La Sagrada Familia is a notable landmark in the city and a must-see place for anybody with an interest in architecture and history. It is an iconic cathedral created by Antoni Gaud.

These are just a handful of the numerous summertime tourist attractions in Barcelona. Whatever your hobbies, this dynamic city is likely to have something to suit you.

The Gothic Quarter is one more summertime hotspot in Barcelona. This historic district is renowned for its old structures, quaint plazas, and winding lanes. It's a wonderful spot to ramble about and discover the history and culture of the city.

The Picasso Museum is a must-see location for art enthusiasts. More than 4,000 pieces of art, including some of the iconic paintings by the well-known artist Pablo Picasso, may be found at this museum, which is devoted to his work.

The Ciutadella Park is an excellent spot to spend a summer day if you're searching for some outdoor entertainment. This large park is the ideal spot to unwind and take in the sunlight since it is home to beautiful gardens, a lake, a fountain, and various museums.

The Barcelona Zoo is another another well-liked summertime tourist attraction. More than 7,000 animals from all around the globe call this well-kept zoo home. It's a terrific location to learn about nature and have some family-friendly fun.

These are just a handful of the numerous summertime tourist attractions in Barcelona. With so much to see and do, it's understandable why this city is a well-liked summer tourist destination.

Proven techniques for discovering inexpensive Barcelona

Book in advance: Book your flights as early as possible, since last-minute reservations tend to be more costly.
Be flexible with travel dates: If feasible, be flexible with your trip dates and aim to fly during off-peak hours, such as midweek or early morning, since these flights are generally cheaper.

Compare pricing: Use online comparison services to compare costs from various airlines. This will give you an idea of the typical price and help you pick the best offer.
Sign up for price notifications: Some websites provide price alerts, which tell you when the price of your selected flight

changes. This might assist you to make a rapid choice if the price reduces.

Use cheap airlines: Budget airlines generally provide reduced fares, but be cautious to evaluate the overall cost including luggage fees and other expenses.

Book a connecting flight: Direct flights are normally more costly than connecting flights, so consider scheduling a connecting trip to save money.

Check for deals and promotions: Airlines regularly conduct sales and promotions, so keep an eye out for them and take advantage of them if feasible.

Join reward programs: Joining an airline loyalty program might provide you access to special deals and discounts.

Try alternate airports: If you're traveling to Barcelona, consider flying to other neighboring airports like Girona or Reus, since flights to these airports may be cheaper.

Use travel points and rewards: If you have acquired travel points or awards, consider using them to book your flights. Many airlines and credit cards provide travel points that may be used for trips.

Book as a group: Booking as a group may often lead to savings on flights, so consider going with friends or family.

Consider other transit: Depending on your trip intentions, consider alternate forms of transportation, such as trains or buses, to reach Barcelona. This may be cheaper and give a unique vacation experience.

Don't overlook hidden charges: When comparing pricing, be sure to take into consideration hidden expenditures such as luggage fees, seat selection fees, and in-flight meals.

Be careful of currency fluctuations: If you're going abroad, be mindful of currency swings and attempt to schedule your flight when the conversion rate is in your favor.

Remember, finding inexpensive tickets to Barcelona might take time and work, but by being flexible and proactive in your search, you can save money and make the most of your vacation.

The cost of using the train around Barcelona

The cost of using the train around Barcelona varies on numerous variables, including the kind of train, the distance traveled, and the time of day. The standard rail price for a single journey on a regional train inside the city is around 2 to 4 euros. If you want to make several excursions, you could consider buying a multi-trip ticket or a tourist pass, which might provide savings. You may consult the official website of the Catalan railway operator, Renfe, for the most up-to-date information on train rates and ticket choices.

The cost of driving or using a cab around Barcelona

The cost of driving or using a cab around Barcelona varies on numerous variables such as the time of day, the distance traveled, and the traffic conditions. On average, a taxi journey in the city center may cost approximately 15-20 euros, while a one-way journey from the airport to the city center can cost around 30-40 euros. If you're driving, you'll need to add in the cost of petrol and parking, which might vary depending on the location and time of day. Some major parking lots in the city might cost roughly 20-30 euros per day. It's always better to study ahead of time and compare costs to get the most cost-effective alternative for your requirements.

If you're driving in Barcelona, it's crucial to be aware of the city's traffic limitations, since many places have limited access to automobiles in order to decrease pollution and encourage sustainable mobility. There are also designated "green zones" where only low-emission cars are permitted. If you've discovered driving a non-compliant car in a prohibited location, you may be liable to a fine.

Taking a cab or utilizing a ride-hailing service like Uber or Cabify is a simple method to travel about Barcelona, particularly if you're unfamiliar with the city or if you have a lot of baggage. Cabs in Barcelona are controlled by the municipal government, and all taxis must have a meter that indicates the cost of the journey. It's usually advisable to hire an official taxi since unlicensed cabs are not regulated and may charge extra.

The cost of driving or taking a cab in Barcelona varies on various aspects, and it's advisable to conduct some research ahead of time to discover the most cost-effective choice for your requirements. Whether you choose to drive or take a cab, be prepared for traffic and plan to guarantee a safe and efficient journey.

Chapter 4: What to know before visiting Barcelona as a first timer

Have some cash at hand as a tourist in Barcelona

As a visitor in Barcelona, it is usually suggested to bring some cash with you. The most extensively used currency in Spain is the Euro (EUR). You may convert your money into Euros at the airport, banks, or exchange bureaus. It's also a good idea to bring a debit or credit card with you since most shops in Barcelona accept card payments, but having cash might come in useful for little purchases or in case of emergencies.

It's always a good idea to have a backup strategy for getting funds. You may consider carrying a debit card or credit card that may be used for cash advances, but be mindful of the costs connected with these transactions.

Consider studying and marking down the locations of local ATMs or banks if you need to withdraw money during your stay.

In Barcelona, it is typical to tip in restaurants and cafés, therefore it's useful to have small sums of cash accessible for this reason. Furthermore, there are street performers and artists who regularly take gratuities, and having some cash on hand might be handy in these instances as well.
Overall, it's better to be prepared with a mix of cash and a debit or credit card when traveling in Barcelona to guarantee that you are ready for any eventuality.

What to know about the Barcelona money before visiting

Before visiting Barcelona, here are some crucial details concerning the money used in the city:

Official currency: The official currency of Barcelona and the rest of Spain is the Euro (EUR) (EUR).

Cash and cards: Both cash and debit/credit cards are frequently accepted in Barcelona, however smaller restaurants and street sellers may only take cash.

ATMs: There are several ATMs accessible in Barcelona that accept major international debit/credit cards. It's a good idea to withdraw cash from ATMs instead of exchanging money at currency exchange offices since they typically offer unfavorable conversion rates.

Tipping: In Barcelona, it's typical to round up the bill to the closest euro while eating out or to leave little change (5-10%) for excellent treatment in a restaurant or taxi/bar services.

Budgeting: Barcelona can be a costly city, particularly for tourist attractions and eating out. It's vital to manage your expenditures and prepare ahead for things like lodgings, transportation, meals, and activities.

Sales Tax: Value Added Tax (VAT) is included in the price of products and services in Spain, with a standard rate of 21%. Some products, such as food and literature, may have a lower VAT rate of 10%.

Credit Card Security: As with any foreign city, it's necessary to be careful of credit card security while using it in Barcelona. Avoid using ATMs in secluded or poorly lit places, and keep an eye on your card and PIN while using them in stores and restaurants.

Exchange Rates: The Euro exchange rate might vary, so it's good to check the current rate before your travel and monitor it throughout your stay. This can help you acquire a better knowledge of the cost of products and budget appropriately.

In conclusion, having a strong grasp of the money used in Barcelona, coupled with budgeting and being cautious of security precautions, can assist guarantee a smooth and pleasurable trip

Have some cash at hand

Were to change money in Barcelona as a tourist

As a guest in Barcelona, you may change money at a currency exchange office, a bank, or an ATM. It's recommended to compare currency rates before completing a purchase to obtain the best value. Some currency exchange bureaus and banks provide greater rates than others. It's also a good idea to research the costs connected with each option before making a selection. Additionally, utilizing ATMs to withdraw local currency is a quick alternative and typically results in reasonable exchange rates, although some institutions may impose fees for foreign transactions.

It is usually suggested to bring a combination of cash and a debit/credit card for your trips. In the event of an emergency, having both solutions ready might be advantageous. When using a debit/credit card, be cautious of the exchange rate and any extra costs that may be levied by your bank for foreign purchases.

It's also crucial to know that certain locations may only take cash, such as street sellers or tiny local stores, so it's always a good idea to have some cash on hand.

When exchanging money, it's a good idea to keep note of the transaction and the amount exchanged to aid with budgeting and to ensure that you don't overspend.

In summary, as a tourist in Barcelona, you have various alternatives for changing money, including currency exchange offices, banks, and ATMs. Be careful to examine exchange rates and costs before making a selection, and consider carrying a

combination of cash and a debit/credit card for your trips
Internet and WiFi

What to know about the Barcelona Sim card proposal for tourist

Barcelona is a famous tourist destination, and many tourists find it beneficial to obtain a local SIM card for their mobile phone during their trip. Here are some crucial points to consider while selecting a SIM card in Barcelona:

Compatibility: Make sure that your mobile phone is compatible with the network technologies used in Spain. Most phones used in Europe and North America are compatible with the GSM network, which is used by all major carriers in Spain.

Operator coverage: Check the coverage maps of several operators to decide which one has the greatest coverage in the regions where you will be staying and traveling.

Data allowance: Consider your data use demands before picking a plan. Some plans give unlimited data, while others may have a data limits or charge for further data consumption.

Cost: Compare the cost of several plans and select one that matches your budget. Some carriers provide prepaid plans, while others may demand a contract.

Convenience: Consider the convenience of acquiring and activating the SIM card. Some carriers have outlets established at the airport, while others may need you to acquire a SIM card at a nearby shop.

Customer service: Make sure the operator offers strong customer service, in case you need help with your SIM card or phone.

Some prominent operators in Spain include Vodafone, Orange, and Movistar. It is suggested to analyze the numerous plans provided by these operators and select one that best matches your demands

International roaming: If you want to go outside of Spain during your vacation, be sure that your SIM card enables international roaming services and verify the cost of using your phone in other countries. Some providers may offer unique deals for international roaming that might save you money.

Prepaid vs. postpaid: Prepaid SIM cards enable you to pay in advance for the services you use, whereas postpaid plans need a contract and charge you at the end of the month. Choose the one that works best for you, depending on your use demands and budget.

4G/LTE services: If you require rapid internet access, consider purchasing a package that provides 4G/LTE services. Most carriers in Spain provide 4G/LTE services, however coverage may vary depending on the location.

Additional services: Some operators may provide additional services, such as unlimited calls to other lines on the same network, savings on international calls, and free roaming in specific countries. Consider these additional services while selecting your SIM card.

buying a local SIM card in Barcelona might be a quick and cost-effective method to remain connected throughout your vacation. By examining the parameters stated above, you may pick the finest SIM card for your requirements.

Multi-SIM options: Some tourists may require numerous SIM cards for their varied gadgets, such as a tablet or a second phone. If this is the case, consider picking an operator that provides multi-SIM possibilities.

Activation procedure: Make sure you understand the activation process for your selected SIM card. Some carriers may ask you to activate the SIM card online, while others may demand you to visit a shop or produce identity papers.

Customer reviews: Before buying a SIM card, read customer reviews to see what other travelers have encountered with the operator and their services. This might help you make an educated selection and prevent any possible complications.

Refunds and returns: In case you change mind or face any troubles with the SIM card, check the operator's policy on refunds and returns. Some operators may have tight requirements, while others may provide more liberal possibilities.

By taking these elements into mind, you can guarantee that you enjoy a seamless and hassle-free experience with your Barcelona SIM card. With a local SIM card, you can remain connected and make the most of your vacation, whether for navigation, communication, or entertainment.

Internet and WiFi usage in Barcelona for tourist

As a visitor in Barcelona, you will have various alternatives for accessing the internet and WiFi. Here are some popular options:

Public WiFi: There are several public WiFi hotspots in Barcelona, including at cafés, restaurants, and hotels. Some big companies like McDonald's and Starbucks also provide free WiFi. However, the quality and speed of these networks might vary and may not be trustworthy.

Cell data: If you have an unlocked smartphone and a valid mobile plan, you may use mobile data while in Barcelona. You may get a local SIM card at a telecoms shop or airport to receive a better cost.

Rent a portable WiFi device: You may rent a portable WiFi device, also known as a pocket WiFi or mobile hotspot, which offers a safe and private connection for numerous devices. You may obtain them for hire at the airport or through local firms.

Hotel WiFi: Many hotels in Barcelona provide free WiFi to visitors, while others have premium choices for faster and more dependable connections for an extra price.

Regardless of the choice you select, it's a good idea to investigate your options in advance and check the evaluations of each provider to ensure that you receive the best possible internet experience while in Barcelona.

It's also crucial to understand that although many public WiFi networks are free, they may not be safe, thus it's not suggested to use them for critical activities like online banking or shopping. When utilizing public WiFi, be sure you utilize a secure VPN provider to safeguard your personal and financial information.

Several major tourist sites in Barcelona, such as the Sagrada Familia and Park Guell, have restricted or no WiFi connectivity, so it may be a good idea to download maps and information before visiting these locations.

Finally, if you need to remain connected for business or other critical affairs, it's suggested to consider obtaining a local SIM card or portable WiFi device, since these alternatives tend to provide more stable and secure connections than public WiFi.

Overall, as a visitor in Barcelona, you have various alternatives for accessing the internet and WiFi, but it's necessary to assess the security and dependability of each service before making a selection. With a little forethought, you can remain connected and make the most of your time in the city.

Another issue to bear in mind when it comes to internet and WiFi access in Barcelona is data use and roaming costs. If you're using your own mobile device and plan, be sure to check with your service provider about any roaming costs or data use limitations that may apply while you're in Barcelona. If you're using a leased portable WiFi device or a local SIM card, be sure you read the terms and conditions of the service, including any data consumption limitations and fees for exceeding such limits.

It's also crucial to note that many cafés, restaurants, and other public areas in Barcelona now provide free charging stations for smartphones and other mobile devices, so you can keep your gadgets fueled up while on the move.

Internet and WiFi connection may be quite beneficial for travelers in Barcelona, enabling you to remain connected, access information, and make the most of your vacation. By studying your choices in advance, keeping data use and roaming costs in mind, and being careful of security while using public WiFi, you may have a smooth and pleasurable online experience while in the city.

Uber and cab in Barcelona

In Barcelona, both Uber and regular taxis are offered as choices for transportation. However, there are some distinctions between the two services.
Uber works as a ridesharing service, where customers may use the Uber app to request transport from private drivers who utilize their cars. This may occasionally result in cheaper pricing than regular taxis, however, the quality of the service might vary.

Traditional taxis in Barcelona are controlled by the city and drivers must hold a taxi license. They may be hailed on the street, hired by phone, or located at taxi stands. Traditional taxis tend to be more costly than Uber, but the service is often more regulated and trustworthy.
Both choices have their benefits and downsides, and the ideal decision for you

will depend on your unique requirements and tastes.

When it comes to convenience, both Uber and regular taxis may be simply hailed or booked in advance. However, with Uber, customers can follow the whereabouts of their driver in real-time and get information about the progress of their journey, which may make the process more transparent and convenient. With regular taxis, you may have to phone the dispatcher or flag one down on the street, and there may be a lengthier wait period, particularly during busy hours.

In terms of safety, both Uber and regular taxis have introduced numerous safety precautions, such as driver background checks and in-app emergency features. However, conventional taxis have a more controlled system for assuring driver and passenger safety, since drivers must comply with tight licensing standards and the cars must undergo frequent inspections.

When it comes to pricing, regular taxis tend to be more costly than Uber, however, costs may vary based on demand, time of day, and other variables. With Uber, customers can see the anticipated price of their journey before they book it, but with conventional taxis, the meter begins running as soon as you get in the vehicle and the price is decided by the distance traveled and time of day.
Both Uber and regular taxis may be a decent option for transportation in Barcelona, but the ideal decision for you will depend on your unique requirements and preferences, such as cost, convenience, and safety
Take the bus or train.

Dietary restrictions and food in Barcelona

Barcelona is a cosmopolitan city with a rich culinary scene, giving several alternatives for persons with various dietary constraints.

For vegans and vegetarians, numerous restaurants provide plant-based food and there are also some specialty vegan/vegetarian eateries.

For people with gluten sensitivity, restaurants are providing gluten-free alternatives and there are also bakeries and shops selling gluten-free items.

For persons with lactose sensitivity, many restaurants feature lactose-free alternatives, and it is also easy to obtain lactose-free dairy products in supermarkets.

Halal food may also be available at various restaurants in the city that provide Middle Eastern and North African cuisine.

Overall, Barcelona has a lot to offer for persons with dietary restrictions and it's very straightforward to discover acceptable solutions.

When it comes to traditional Catalan cuisine, meals like paella, tapas, and calçots are popular. Many of these meals may be modified to fit dietary requirements, but it's always better to check with the restaurant ahead.

the city boasts a bustling street food culture, with food trucks and booths providing a variety of alternatives, including vegan and vegetarian options, such as falafel, veggie burgers, and plant-based tacos.
Barcelona is a food-friendly city that accommodates to a range of dietary needs. Whether you're seeking traditional Catalan food, vegan alternatives, or gluten-free options, there is something for everyone. With a little bit of study and forethought, it is simple to enjoy the city's great cuisine without sacrificing your dietary demands.

Be careful in Barcelona as a tourist

As with any city, it is recommended for tourists visiting Barcelona practice care and be aware of their surroundings. Here are a few ideas to assist guarantee a safe and happy trip:

Keep valuables (such as passports, money, and credit cards) in a secure location and avoid flashing big quantities of cash.

Be careful of pickpocketing, particularly in busy locations like the subway, tourist spots, and markets.

Avoid going alone at night in poorly lit or uninhabited locations.

Be wary while using ATMs, since card skimming is a widespread occurrence.

Be conscious of local laws and traditions to prevent inadvertent cultural misunderstandings.

Always carry a charged cell phone in case of emergencies.

By following these recommendations and exercising common sense, travelers may help guarantee a safe and happy vacation to Barcelona.

Use of English in Barcelona.

English is extensively spoken in Barcelona as a second language, notably in the tourism business. Most hotels, restaurants, and businesses will have workers who can speak English, making it easier for guests to converse and move about the city. However, it is always welcome to attempt to speak Spanish, since it demonstrates respect for the local culture.
Additionally, many street signs, restaurants, and tourist information are provided in both Spanish and English. This makes it easier for English-speaking guests to explore the city and locate what they need. However, it is still a good idea to acquire a basic grasp of Spanish, as it may aid in talking with local folks, particularly in more rural or less tourist locations.

English is very extensively used among foreign tourists in Barcelona, thus it is feasible to converse with people in the same language. However, tourists are advised to immerse themselves in the local culture by practicing their Spanish and acquiring certain crucial words.

In conclusion, although English is commonly spoken in Barcelona, it is still a good idea to have a basic grasp of Spanish and to make an attempt to converse in the local language. This will not only improve your vacation experience but also show respect for the local culture

Weekend activities in Barcelona

Here are some popular weekend activities in Barcelona:

Visit the magnificent Sagrada Familia
Walk around the Gothic Quarter and explore its street art and architecture

Explore Park Guell and its mosaics built by Antoni Gaudi
Check out the Picasso Museum
Stroll along La Rambla, a lively promenade crowded with street performers and merchants
Visit the Joan Miro Foundation to view modern and contemporary art
Enjoy the local food at La Boqueria market
Visit the Gothic Cathedral of Barcelona
Take a day excursion to Montserrat Monastery
Enjoy the Mediterranean beaches and nightlife of Barceloneta.
Note: Some of these attractions may have restricted capacity or be closed due to COVID-19. Please verify before visiting.

There are various cultural activities that you may enjoy in Barcelona:

Attend a flamenco concert to appreciate the classic Spanish dance

Visit the Palau de la Musica Catalana to attend a classical music performance

Explore the National Art Museum of Catalonia (MNAC) to explore the works of local and international artists

Visit the Fundació Joan Miró to view the paintings of the renowned Surrealist artist

Take a cooking lesson to learn how to create traditional Catalan cuisine.

Barcelona also provides various outdoor activities for individuals who enjoy the outdoors:

Go for a bike ride along the beachside promenade

Visit the Parc de la Ciutadella for a picnic or relax in the park

Take a spectacular hot air balloon trip for a bird's eye perspective over the city

Visit the Zoo de Barcelona to witness a variety of animals

Take a picturesque boat cruise to observe the city's coastline and beaches.

Whether you enjoy indoor or outdoor activities, art or nature, Barcelona has plenty to offer everyone. Enjoy your weekend

Top 10 money-saving tips in Barcelona

Use public transportation: The metro and bus system in Barcelona are efficient and cost-effective ways to get around.
Walk: Walking is a terrific way to experience the city and save money on transportation.
Eat like a local: Try traditional Spanish foods at local pubs and cafés, which are generally less costly than tourist establishments.
Avoid tourist traps: Touristy locations frequently offer higher rates, so explore neighboring neighborhoods to locate more cheaply priced choices.

Buy food at markets: Fresh fruit, meats, and cheeses may be obtained at local markets cheaper than in restaurants.

Use tap water: Barcelona has great tap water, so pack a reusable bottle and replenish it during the day instead of purchasing bottled water.

Take advantage of free attractions: Numerous museums and galleries provide free entry on certain days of the week, and there are also many parks and gardens to explore.

Book lodgings in advance: Booking in advance may frequently result in reduced pricing for hotels and flats.

Tourists' favorite summertime destination in Barcelona

Shop at bargain stores: Stores like Primark and H&M provide low-priced apparel and accessories, and there are also several street markets offering used products.

Chapter 5:
Do's and don't of staying safe in Barcelona
Barcelona Safety Do's & Don'ts

DO'S :

Research the area before you go, particularly if it's your first time in Barcelona.

Respect local traditions and laws.
Have a map or GPS with you to help you navigate the city.

Keep valuables in a secure place and be aware of pick-pocketing, particularly in busy situations.

Stay in well-lit and busy settings, particularly at night.

Be cautious when using ATMs, since card skimming is common.

Familiarize yourself with local emergency numbers and procedures.

Drink lots of water and maintain hydrated, particularly in the heat.

DON'TS:

Don't flaunt valuables or big sums of cash in public.

Don't leave your valuables unattended or visible in a vehicle.

Don't accept drinks from strangers or leave your drink unattended.

Don't walk alone in lonely or poorly illuminated regions.

Don't engage with aggressive or persistent street salespeople.

Don't partake in unlawful activities, such as drug usage or theft.

Don't disregard traffic signals and restrictions, particularly while crossing the street.

Don't wear clothes or carry anything that can make you a target for theft or harassment.

It's crucial to note that by adopting common sense safety methods and being aware of your surroundings, you may greatly minimize your chance of encountering danger when in Barcelona.

Mingle with Barcelonans

How to connect with Barcelonans as a tourist

Here are some recommendations to mingle with locals in Barcelona:
Learn some easy Spanish phrases to demonstrate your interest in the local language and culture.

Visit local markets, cafés, and bars to witness and interact with the everyday lives of people.

Join a walking tour guided by a local guide to obtaining an insight into the city's history and culture.

Attend local festivals and events to obtain a sense of the city's traditions and customs.

Take part in local activities such as playing football or going on a walk to meet residents who have similar interests.

Be alert to local customs and traditions, and try to avoid touristic sites.

Engage in relationships with people, ask questions, and be open to learning about their culture and way of life.

Do not be scared to ask questions
As a guest in Barcelona, it is appropriate to ask inquiries. The local folks are kind and frequently willing to serve visitors. You may ask for directions, suggestions for restaurants or activities, or information about public transit. Don't hesitate to ask for assistance, since it is the greatest way to make the most of your visit to the city.

Obey their laws
Driving: If you're driving, it's crucial to be informed of the local traffic rules, including speed limits and limitations on mobile phone usage while going.

Remember, breaching the law may result in fines, jail, or other legal repercussions, so it's crucial to be aware and obey the regulations.

Additionally, it's crucial to respect the local culture and customs. Barcelona is a city with a rich history and cultural legacy, so it's vital to be conscious of your conduct and appearance in public areas, especially around religious sites and museums.

Also, be considerate to the local population by avoiding noisy and disruptive conduct in residential neighborhoods, particularly late at night.
Lastly, be sure to carry identification with you at all times, since the authorities may want to examine it if they suspect any illegal conduct.

In conclusion, by obeying the rules and respecting the local culture, you may ensure a safe and pleasurable vacation to Barcelona. If you have any queries or

worries, don't hesitate to approach a local or tourist information center for help
Pharmacies
First aid

In case of an emergency when traveling in Barcelona, you should:

Call 112 (European emergency number) for any medical, fire, or police issues.
Locate the closest hospital, which may be identified using internet maps or by asking locals.
If you need non-emergency medical treatment, you may visit a local pharmacy (farmacia) and ask for help.
If you have a pre-existing medical condition, please be sure to take appropriate medicines and medical paperwork with you.
Make sure you keep travel insurance information with you at all times.
It is also essential to educate oneself with basic first aid procedures, such as CPR, and

to acquire a few important words in Spanish for speaking with local medical personnel.

Below are a few typical health conditions you may experience when traveling and advice for avoiding or treating them:

Dehydration: Stay hydrated by drinking lots of water, particularly during hot weather. Avoid sugary or caffeinated beverages.

Sunburn: Protect your skin from the sun by wearing a hat, and sunglasses, and using sunscreen with a high SPF.

Motion sickness: If you're prone to motion sickness, try taking over-the-counter medicine before traveling and sitting in a seat facing the front of the car.

Food poisoning: Eat at reputed restaurants and avoid street food that has been hanging out in the sun. Make careful to wash your hands periodically and only drink bottled water.

Insect bites: Use insect repellent and wear long sleeves and trousers in the evenings to prevent mosquito bites.

Remember, being prepared and knowledgeable may make a great difference in ensuring a safe and healthy journey.

Careful when crossing the road in Barcelona

In Barcelona, it is particularly vital to remain alert while crossing major highways or crossroads. Drivers in the city might be fast and aggressive, and may not always give precedence to pedestrians. To keep safe, it is a good idea to cross the road at authorized pedestrian crossings and to wait for a break in traffic before crossing. It is also a good idea to avoid distractions such as using your phone or listening to music with headphones when crossing the road since these might hinder your ability to hear incoming cars.

Additionally, it is necessary to be aware of the local road signs and traffic signals, since they may vary from those in your native country. For example, in certain districts of Barcelona, pedestrians are forced to cross the road at designated crossing places and may be punished for crossing outside of these zones. By familiarizing yourself with the local traffic regulations and practices, you can guarantee that you remain safe while crossing the road in Barcelona.

In conclusion, crossing the road in Barcelona demands a heightened degree of care and awareness, but with a little bit of additional attention and caution, you can remain safe and enjoy your visit to this wonderful city.

Avoid night movement as the first timer in Barcelona

As a safety precaution, it is advisable to avoid wandering alone in unknown regions or during late night hours while visiting a new city like Barcelona. This may lessen the chance of theft or other illicit activity. Instead, it is advised to select well-lit and busy places and consider utilizing public transit or taxi services during late hours.

It is also crucial to be mindful of your surroundings and keep precious objects protected. When strolling in unfamiliar regions, avoid wearing headphones or gazing at your phone for lengthy periods, since this might make you a target for pickpockets.

Additionally, it is usually important to acquaint oneself with the local emergency services and know how to call them if required. Make sure to keep a charged cell phone and important papers, such as your passport or ID, with you at all times.

Barcelona is a dynamic and interesting city, but like any other metropolitan area, it is vital to take care to keep it safe. By following these easy rules and being careful of your surroundings, you may assure a safe and pleasant vacation to Barcelona.

Chapter 6:
Making friends with Barcelona locals as a tourist

As a visitor, you may establish friends with Barcelona natives by:

Participating in local activities and events, such as festivals, sports tournaments, or cultural performances.

Joining organizations or groups that fit with your hobbies, such as hiking, photography, or cooking.

Volunteering or engaging in community service initiatives.

Taking lessons or courses that enable you to engage with locals, such as language classes or cookery classes.

Staying at local lodgings, such as hostels or Airbnb, which may allow the opportunity to engage with locals and other tourists.

Spending time at local cafés, pubs, or restaurants, which are fantastic venues to meet people and start discussions.

Being open and welcoming, demonstrating an interest in the local culture, and respect for local traditions.

By following these recommendations, you may create true relationships with locals and have an authentic experience in Barcelona.

Participating in tours given by local guides who may offer insight into the city's history, culture, and customs.

Engaging with local artists and creatives, for example, by visiting local galleries, studios, or markets.

Exploring the city's areas and seeking chances to connect with locals, such as conversing with merchants or starting up discussions with individuals in parks or public places.

Asking locals for suggestions and advice, such as the finest places to eat, drink, or visit.

Using social media and internet channels to interact with locals, such as local Facebook groups or Meetup groups.

Remember, building friends with locals is a two-way street, so be open to developing real friendships and learning from each other. Be courteous, interested, and genuine, and you will discover that residents are frequently eager to welcome tourists and share their city with them.

Is Barcelona's population pleasant and hospitable?

Yes, generally speaking, people in Barcelona are recognized for being polite and accommodating. The city has a rich culture, history, and varied people, making it an inviting site for tourists. People in Barcelona are proud of their city and are willing to share their culture and customs with anyone who is interested.

The hospitality business is highly developed in Barcelona, with numerous hotels, restaurants, and pubs giving good service to guests. Tourists may expect to be greeted with warmth and respect, and locals are typically willing to assist you with directions or ideas for things to see and do in the city.

Barcelona is also a city with a strong feeling of community, and this is reflected in the way that people connect. Whether it's starting up a conversation with a stranger at a café or helping a lost visitor find their way, folks in Barcelona are recognized for being friendly and accessible.

In summary, Barcelona is a city with a warm and cordial attitude, and tourists can expect to feel at home as they discover everything that the city has to offer

How to engage with Barcelonians as a tourist

As a visitor in Barcelona, you might attempt to interact with the locals by following these tips:

Learn a few Spanish phrases and practice speaking the language with locals.

Visit local markets, parks, and plazas to experience everyday life and observe local traditions.
Try local gastronomy, such as tapas, paella, and other traditional specialties.

Explore the city's cultural sites, museums, and theaters to obtain a deeper grasp of the city's history and arts.
Participate in local events and festivals, such as the La Mercè festival, which is a great celebration of music, dancing, and cuisine in the city.

Join a walking tour or attend a culinary class to learn more about the local culture and meet other visitors and locals.

Lastly, be respectful of the local customs and traditions and always ask before snapping pictures of people.

How to approach a Barcelonian

When approaching a native as a visitor in Barcelona, it's crucial to be courteous and observant of their culture. Here are some suggestions to assist you:

Learn a few fundamental words in Spanish: Saying "Hola" (hello) and "Gracias" (thank you) may go a far way in demonstrating your appreciation for the local culture.

Dress appropriately: Avoid wearing exposing attire and be cognizant of local norms and traditions.

Be nice and friendly: Smile and establish eye contact while conversing with natives. Ask for assistance or instructions respectfully.

Respect personal space: Avoid going too near or breaching personal space, particularly in busy situations.
Don't litter: Keep the city clean and dispose of your rubbish correctly.

By following these easy guidelines, you may create a favorable impression on the locals and have a more genuine and pleasurable time in Barcelona

Barcelona Tourist Phrases

Hola/Bon dia (Hello/Good morning)

Com estas? (How are you?)

Gràcies (Thank you)

Si us plau (Please)

Disculpi (Excuse me)

Parles anglès? (Do you speak English?)

On és …? (Where is …?)

Quant val? (How much does it cost?)

No entenc (I don't understand)

De on ets? (Where are you from?)

Chapter 7 Best Relaxation and massage center in Barcelona

highly recommended massage centers in Barcelona

1.MSPAclic - A top-rated spa with a variety of massages, facials, and body treatments to choose from.

2.Spa Zenit - This luxurious spa features a range of massages, beauty treatments, and a heated pool.

3.Omm Spa - Known for its contemporary design and high-quality treatments, Omm Spa is a popular choice for those seeking relaxation and rejuvenation

4.Baños Árabes - Offering a traditional hammam experience, this spa features a range of massages and beauty treatments inspired by ancient Arab bathhouses.

5.Chill Out Spa - Specializing in Thai massage, this spa is a great choice for those seeking a more exotic and authentic spa experience.

All these spas offer great services and it's a matter of personal preference, I would recommend checking their websites or calling ahead to book an appointment, as availability can vary.

When visiting any of these spas, you can expect a calming and peaceful atmosphere, as well as professional and knowledgeable therapists who will provide a personalized experience. Some spas also offer additional services such as a sauna, steam room, or hot tub to further enhance your relaxation. It is always a good idea to inform the spa in advance of any specific needs or preferences you have, such as any health conditions or areas you would like them to focus on during your massage.

In Barcelona, many spas also offer packages that combine multiple treatments into a full day of pampering and relaxation. This can be a great option if you're looking to fully immerse yourself in the spa experience.

No matter which spa you choose, a massage or relaxation treatment in Barcelona is sure to be a highlight of your trip. So take some time for yourself, and indulge in some much-needed pampering and rejuvenation.

Chapter 8: Top Barcelona museums

Here are some of the top museums in Barcelona, Spain:

best museums in the city of Barcelona

Picasso Museum: The largest collection of
Pablo Picasso's artwork is housed in this museum, which is devoted to the artist's

work:

Paintings, sculptures, and other pieces of art from the Middle Ages to the present day can be found at the Museu Nacional d'Art de Catalunya.

Fundació Joan Miró: This museum showcases a variety of the Catalan artist's paintings, sculptures, and other creations and is devoted to his body of work.

Museu Historia de Barcelona: This museum is devoted to the history of the city and contains artifacts from more recent history as well as the Roman and medieval eras.

Museu d'Arqueologia de Catalunya:

This museum showcases a collection of artifacts from ancient civilizations like the Romans, Greeks, and Etruscans. It is devoted to the archaeology of Catalonia.

Museu d'Art Contemporani de Barcelona:

This museum specializes in contemporary art and exhibits creations by international artists.

CosmoCaixa

is a science museum withexhibits covering a variety of subjects, such as biology, space exploration, and theenvironment.

Museu Martim: This museum showcases a collection of ships and other maritime artifacts and is devoted to the history of the sea and shipping.

Fundació Antoni Tàpies: This museum showcases the creations of Catalan artist Antoni Tàpies, who is well-known for his abstract sculptures and paintings.
Dedicated to ancient Egyptian culture, the

Museu Egipci de Barcelona houses a variety of artifacts and exhibits on the civilization's history and religion.

Fundació Suol: This gallery exhibits works by international artists and is devoted to contemporary art.

The Museu de la Xocolata is a museum that is devoted to the art and history of making.

Chocolate. It offers exhibits on the history and production of chocolate, as well as tastings and demonstrations.

Museu del Modernisme: This museum is

dedicated to Catalonia's Modernist

movement and houses a variety of artwork,

furniture, and other items from that time.

The Museu de la Música is a museum devoted to the study of music history. It displays the development of musical instruments as well as the background of various musical genres.

The Museu de la Ciència is a science museum with interactive displays on a variety of scientific subjects, such as physics,biology, and chemistry.

These are only a few of Barcelona's

numerous worthwhile museums. You can find a museum in the city that will interest you no matter what your interests are.

Chapter 9: Top hotels and beaches in Barcelona

Barcelona is a lively city with a rich history and culture, and it provides a broad selection of hotels for tourists. The Mandarin Oriental, Barcelona is one of the most luxurious hotels in the city, offering spectacular views of the city and the Mediterranean. It's a fantastic option for people who wish to enjoy the city's best facilities.

W Barcelona is another prominent hotel, recognized for its contemporary style and panoramic views of the city. This hotel is situated on the beach and has a beautiful spa, rooftop patio, and various restaurants.

Casa Fuster is a historic hotel that has been wonderfully restored to its original Art Nouveau form. This hotel is in the center of the city, near the Passeig de Gracia, and gives convenient access to the city's top shopping, eating, and cultural activities.

The Fairmont Rey Juan Carlos I is a huge hotel on a hilltop on the outskirts of Barcelona. This hotel offers stunning views of the city and the Mediterranean and features a golf course, several swimming pools, and a spa.

The Majestic Hotel & Spa Barcelona is a grand hotel in the heart of the city. This hotel features a rooftop terrace with views of the city and the sea, as well as a luxurious spa and several dining options.

Barcelona is also home to several stunning beaches, including Barceloneta Beach, which is one of the most popular in the city. This beach is in the heart of the city and offers a lively atmosphere, with plenty of restaurants, bars, and shops nearby.
Icaria Beach and Nova Icaria Beach are both located in the Olympic Marina area of

the city and are known for their clean sands and clear waters. These beaches are popular with families, and there are plenty of amenities nearby, including restaurants, bars, and shops.

Mar Bella Beach is a famous beach located in the Sant Marti district of the city, and it is known for its lively atmosphere and clean sand. This beach is popular with younger travelers, and there are plenty of restaurants, bars, and shops nearby.

Bogatell Beach is a popular beach in the Poblenou district of the city, and it is known for its clean sand and clear waters. This beach is a popular spot for families, and there are plenty of amenities nearby, including restaurants, bars, and shops.

Aside from its fancy hotels and lovely beaches, Barcelona is also recognized for its rich cultural legacy. The city is home to numerous world-famous monuments, including the Sagrada Familia, Park Guell, Casa Batllo, and the Gothic Quarter. These well-known sites draw millions of visitors every year, making Barcelona one of the most popular destinations in Europe.

Besides its cultural attractions, Barcelona is also known for its gastronomy, which boasts a blend of traditional Catalan specialties and cosmopolitan tastes. The city is home to several eateries, ranging from modest tapas bars to upmarket dining venues. Whether you're searching for fresh seafood, substantial stews, or sweet pastries, there's something for everyone in Barcelona's culinary scene.

When it comes to shopping, Barcelona is a shopper's paradise, featuring a vast choice of shops, marketplaces, and shopping malls. The city is home to numerous huge shopping complexes, notably El Corte Ingles, as well as many smaller stores that provide unique and handcrafted things.

Whether you're seeking For fashionable apparel, jewelry, or local crafts, you will find what you're looking for in Barcelona.

In conclusion, Barcelona is a very unique city that provides something to everyone. Whether you're seeking for luxurious hotels, stunning beaches, world-class cultural activities, wonderful cuisine, or fantastic shopping, Barcelona offers it all. It's little surprise that so many visitors rush to this city every year to see its many delights for themselves.

Chapter 10: Top Barcelona tourist attraction

Some of the top tourist attractions in Barcelona, Spain include:

La Sagrada Familia
La Sagrada Familia is one of the top tourist attractions in Barcelona. It is a large, unfinished Roman Catholic basilica designed by Spanish architect Antoni Gaudi.

Other popular tourist attractions in Barcelona include Park Güell, Casa Batlló, and La Pedrera, also designed by Antoni Gaudi; the Gothic Quarter, a historic neighborhood filled with narrow streets, quaint plazas, and medieval buildings; the Picasso Museum, which houses one of the largest collections of the artist's works; and the Camp Nou, the stadium of Barcelona Football Club, one of the most successful and popular soccer teams in the world. The beaches of Barceloneta, Passeig de Gracia, and the vibrant food scene are also highlights for visitors to the city.

Other notable attractions in Barcelona include the Joan Miro Foundation, showcasing the works of the famous Catalan artist; the Palace of Catalan Music, a beautiful concert hall with an ornate interior; and the Columbus Monument, a tall column with a statue of Christopher Columbus at the top, located in the harbor near La Rambla. Montjuïc Castle, a military fortress located on a hill overlooking the city, offers panoramic views of Barcelona and the surrounding area. The nearby Gothic Quarter is also popular for its shops, bars, and restaurants, making it a great place to spend an evening. With so many unique and interesting places to visit, Barcelona is a city that offers something for everyone, making it one of the most popular tourist destinations in Europe.

For those interested in history and culture, Barcelona is home to many museums and galleries, including the National Art Museum of Catalonia, the Museum of the History of Barcelona, and the Ceramic Museum of Barcelona. The city is also known for its modernist architecture, with buildings by Antoni Gaudi and other architects such as Joan Rubió, Lluís Domènech i Montaner, and Josep Puig i Cadafalch. There are many festivals and events held throughout the year, such as the Barcelona International Jazz Festival, the Barcelona Beach Festival, and La Mercè, the city's main festival, which takes place in late September and features a variety of performances, parades, and concerts. With so much to see and do, it is no wonder that Barcelona attracts millions of visitors every year.

Printed in Great Britain
by Amazon